Tim Howard

By Jon M. Fishman

AMAZING ATHLETES

Lerner Publications • Minneapolis

Lerner Publications Company
A division of Lerner Publishing Group, Inc.
241 First Avenue North
Minneapolis, MN 55401 USA

For reading levels and more information, look up this title at www.lernerbooks.com.

Library of Congress Cataloging-in-Publication Data

Cataloging-in-Publication Data for *Tim Howard* is on file at the Library of Congress.
ISBN: 978-1-4677-5746-1 (lib. bdg.: alk. paper)
ISBN: 978-1-4677-6057-7 (pbk.)
ISBN: 978-1-4677-6214-4 (EB pdf)

Manufactured in the United States of America
1 – BP – 12/31/14

TABLE OF CONTENTS

Tim Howard defends the goal during a 2014 World Cup match against Belgium.

USA STOPPER

US **goalkeeper** Tim Howard shuffled to his left. His eyes were locked on the soccer ball. He moved as the ball moved. The Belgian national team raced up the field. Their bright red uniforms flashed in front of Tim's eyes. But he stayed focused on the ball.

Tim and the US men's soccer team were playing against Belgium on July 1, 2014. The World Cup match was held in Salvador, Brazil. Thousands of excited fans at the arena cheered and clapped. Millions of people all around the world watched the match on TV.

Fans cheer at the 2014 World Cup game between the United States and Belgium.

Divock Origi, a Belgian player, broke into the open with the ball. Tim was already moving. He bent his knees and stayed low to the ground. He spread his big, gloved hands to cover as much of the goal as possible.

Origi fired the ball toward the goal. Tim lashed out with his right leg and kicked the

Tim (1) blocks a shot by Divock Origi (17) of the Belgian team.

ball off the field. It was Tim's first **save** of the match. He had stopped a great shot by Belgium.

Most people expected Belgium to win the match. They were one of the top-ranked teams in the world. The Belgians fired shot after shot at the goal. But Tim always made the save. He dove to his left and to his right, slapping the ball away. He leaped to poke the ball. He punched the ball away with two fists.

Tim tips an oncoming ball up over the goal.

Tim and his ex-wife, Laura, have two kids. Their son, Jacob, is eight years old, and their daughter, Ali, is seven years old.

Neither team could score in the first half. In the second half, Belgium continued to shower Tim with shots. Fans of both teams were getting nervous. When time ran out on the second half, the score was still tied, 0–0. The match would go to **extra time**.

The Belgians pounded Tim with

Tim blocked 16 out of 18 shots on goal in the 2014 US-Belgium World Cup game.

Some fans painted their faces to support the US men's soccer team at the 2014 World Cup.

shots. But they couldn't score. Finally, Belgium broke through and scored twice. They won the match, 2–1.

Despite his team's loss, Tim had put on one of the most incredible goalkeeping displays the world had ever seen. His 16 saves against Belgium set a new World Cup record for the most saves in a single game.

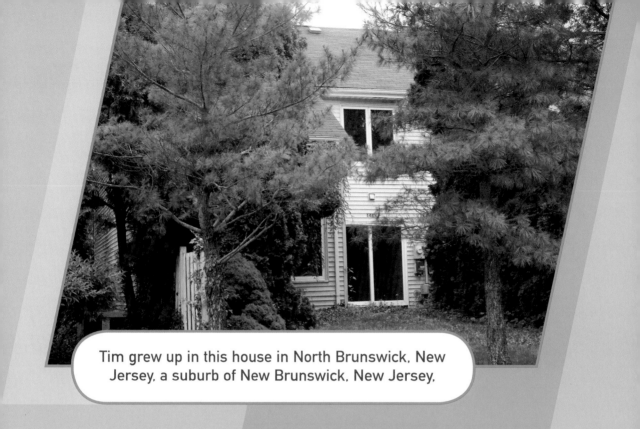

Tim grew up in this house in North Brunswick, New Jersey, a suburb of New Brunswick, New Jersey,

"TIM WHO SCORED GOALS"

Timothy Matthew Howard was born on March 6, 1979, in North Brunswick, New Jersey. He has an older brother named Chris. Their parents, Esther and Matthew, divorced when Tim was three years old. Chris and Tim lived with their mother.

Esther raised the two boys on her own. "It certainly wasn't easy, but the three of us were very, very close," she said. Tim and his brother loved to play sports. But team uniforms and trips to tournaments were expensive. Esther often worked two jobs to keep up with the costs.

Tim liked to play baseball and basketball. But his favorite sport was soccer. From the beginning, he stood out on the soccer field.

North Brunswick is in northern New Jersey, not far from New York City.

Tim's mom, Esther, was a devoted mother to her two sons.

Tim Mulqueen was Howard's youth soccer coach.

Tim Mulqueen coached Tim on a youth soccer team. "Even at a young age, at 12, 13, 14, he was different," Coach Mulqueen said of Tim. "He was better than the kids [who were] older than him."

When Tim was in sixth grade, his mother became worried about him. He sometimes had **tics** that he couldn't control. Doctors told the Howards that Tim had **Tourette syndrome**. This is a serious condition that makes it hard for people to control their movements. Some people also make sounds that they can't stop.

Tim didn't let Tourette syndrome keep him from doing the things he wanted to do. He looked at the condition as a challenge to overcome. Playing sports helped. Tim could focus on the game and not worry about anything else. "On the field I wasn't Tim who had [Tourette syndrome] or Tim who had tics," he said. "I was Tim who scored goals or scored baskets or hit home runs."

Tim Howard (*right*) plays soccer in high school.

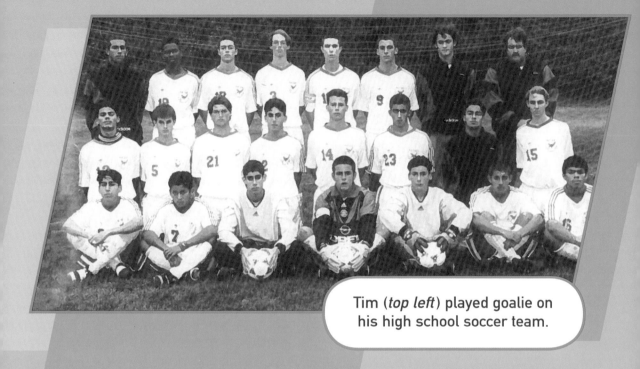

Tim (*top left*) played goalie on his high school soccer team.

MOVING QUICKLY

Tim was a senior at North Brunswick Township High School in 1997. He led the school's basketball team to victory in the **conference** tournament that year. But his heart was with soccer. He had dreams of playing soccer professionally after high school.

Tim Mulqueen, Tim's youth soccer coach, became the head coach of the North Jersey Imperials soccer team in 1997. The Imperials were a professional squad that played in the United Soccer Leagues. Coach Mulqueen brought Tim to the Imperials to play goalkeeper.

It wasn't long before Tim showed he was too good to stay with the Imperials. He moved up to play with the New York/New Jersey MetroStars after just six games. The team is part of Major League Soccer (MLS). MLS is the biggest soccer league in the United States.

Tim was named Most Athletic in his high school yearbook.

Tim didn't get to play much at first. In fact, Tim played in just one MetroStars game in 1998. But he soon began to prove himself. He played in nine games in 1999 and nine more in 2000.

In 2006, the New York/New Jersey MetroStars changed the team name to the New York Red Bulls.

The MetroStars liked what they saw in Tim. The team traded away starting goalkeeper Mike Ammann before the start of the 2001 season. The move left the starting job open for Tim to take.

Tim was ready. He allowed just 35 goals in 26 games in 2001. In four games, he kept the other team from scoring even one goal! That meant he notched four **clean sheets**. Tim was named MLS Goalkeeper of the Year when the season ended.

Soccer teams and fans all around the world noticed Tim's great goalkeeping. In 2003, Tim

Tim (*left*) stops a shot on goal by a D.C. United player.

agreed to join Manchester United (Man U). Man U plays in the **Premier League** in England. The team is one of the most successful pro soccer teams in the world. "Players work hard every day for the hope to have this kind of opportunity," Tim said. The team signed him to a **contract** worth millions of dollars. Tim was rich!

Tim celebrates after signing the contract to join the Man U soccer team.

PREMIER GOALKEEPER

Tim stood tall in his first matches in the English Premier League. But playing for Man U is a difficult job. Fans expect the team to win every game. Tim allowed a goal that fans and coaches thought he should have stopped. It cost his team a big match. During the next two seasons, Tim spent a lot of time on the bench.

Man U sent Tim to Everton Football Club before the start of the 2006–2007 season. Everton is also in the Premier League. Tim was excited about the move. He could have a fresh start. "It was my new lease on life," he said. Tim was sure he could hold down the starting job with his new team.

Before Tim began playing for Everton, he joined the United States team at the 2006 World Cup in Germany.

In 2014, *Forbes* magazine named Manchester United the third most valuable sports team in the world.

Tim (*center*) snatches the ball during a Premier League match.

The World Cup is the biggest soccer event on Earth. It is held once every four years to determine a world champion. Tim was excited to go.

Tim served as the backup to starting goalkeeper Kasey Keller. Tim didn't play in any of the games. But being with Team USA in

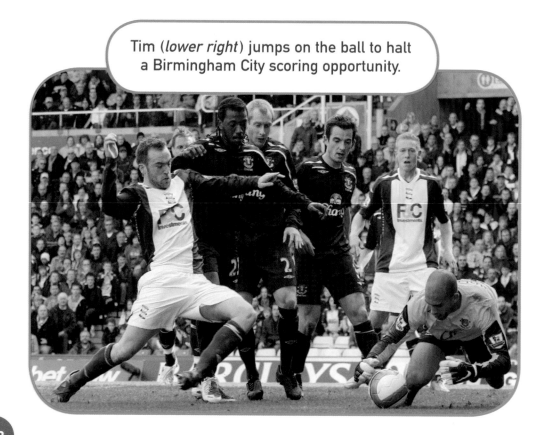

Tim (*lower right*) jumps on the ball to halt a Birmingham City scoring opportunity.

Germany was a valuable experience. He learned what it takes to succeed at the world's biggest soccer tournament. He vowed to be the team's starting goalkeeper at the 2010 World Cup.

Over the next few years, Tim excelled with Everton. He had racked up 45 clean sheets with the team by the end of the 2009–2010 season. Tim's tough days with Man U were behind him. He was one of the top goalkeepers in the Premier League and the world.

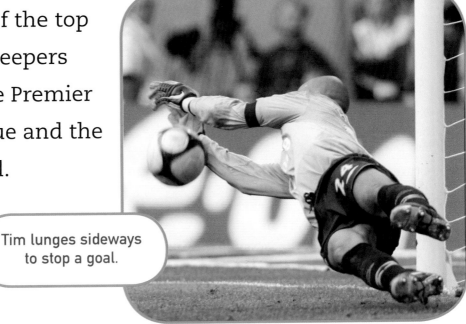

Tim lunges sideways to stop a goal.

In 2010, Tim was named starting goalkeeper for the United States for the 2010 World Cup. He had met his goal. The tournament was held in South Africa. The United States fought to **draws** with England and Slovenia. Then Tim kept a clean sheet to help beat Algeria, 1–0.

Tim (*left*) punches the ball away from the goal in a 2010 World Cup game against Slovenia.

Asamoah Gyan (3) slips the ball past Tim, winning the game for Ghana.

The United States faced Ghana next. The match went to extra time. But Ghana came out on top, 2–1.

After the 2010 World Cup, Tim returned to play for Everton. He continued to be one of the best goalies in the Premier League. By 2014, he had racked up 102 clean sheets with the club.

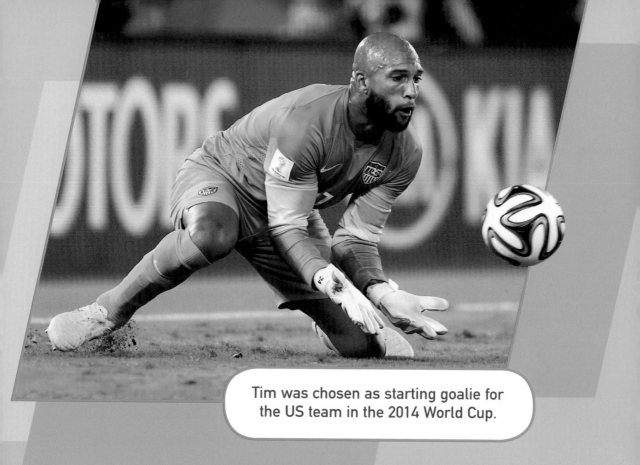

Tim was chosen as starting goalie for the US team in the 2014 World Cup.

AMERICAN HERO

In May 2014, the United States team named Tim the starting goalkeeper for the 2014 World Cup in Brazil. The team's first match was against Ghana. The United States wanted revenge for losing to Ghana in 2010. Team USA came roaring onto the **pitch**. They scored their first goal in just 29 seconds. The United States won the match, 2–1.

Portugal was next up for the United States. The Portuguese team was highly ranked and packed full of superstars. Team USA held a one-goal lead in extra time. But Portugal scored with only a few seconds left.

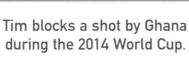

Tim blocks a shot by Ghana during the 2014 World Cup.

Tim grabs the ball away from a Portugal player in the 2014 World Cup.

The match ended in a draw.

The United States next faced Germany in a rainy match. Germany came out on top, 1–0. But the United States had enough points in the first round to advance to the second stage of the World Cup. In that stage, Belgium defeated Team USA.

Though the United States lost, Tim's impressive display of skill at the World Cup made him one of the hottest sports stars in the

United States. He appeared on national TV shows such as *CBS This Morning*. He and teammate Clint Dempsey even got a phone call from President Obama. "You guys did us proud," the president told the pair.

Germany went on to beat Argentina in the final match of the 2014 World Cup. It was the fourth time Germany had won the tournament.

Soccer fans went nuts for Tim during the 2014 World Cup.

Tim signs autographs for fans.

Tim has said that he doesn't see himself playing soccer beyond the age of 40. "There are other things I want to achieve in life, other things that I want to do," he said. He'll be 39 years old when the World Cup comes around again in 2018. Soccer fans hope Tim will take one more run at the world championship.

Selected Career Highlights

2013–2014 Set a World Cup record with 16 saves in one match
Tallied 113 saves and 15 clean sheets with Everton

2012–2013 Tallied 90 saves and 10 clean sheets with Everton

2011–2012 Tallied 95 saves and 12 clean sheets with Everton

2010–2011 Tallied 100 saves and 9 clean sheets with Everton

2009–2010 Tallied 114 saves and 11 clean sheets with Everton
Served as the starting goalkeeper for the United States
at the World Cup

2008–2009 Tallied 114 saves and 17 clean sheets with Everton

2007–2008 Tallied 89 saves and 14 clean sheets with Everton

2006–2007 Moved to Everton Football Club
Tallied 134 saves and 14 clean sheets with Everton

2005–2006 Benched for most of the season after making several errors

2004–2005 Was in and out of the starting lineup for Manchester United

2003–2004 Named Goalkeeper of the Year in England
Joined Manchester United of the English Premier League
Allowed 18 goals in 13 games with the MetroStars

2002 Allowed 44 goals in 27 games with the MetroStars

2001 Allowed 35 goals in 26 games with the MetroStars
Named MLS Goalkeeper of the Year
Named New York Life Humanitarian of the Year for
work spreading Tourette syndrome awareness

2000 Allowed 14 goals in nine games with the MetroStars

1999 Allowed 13 goals in nine games with the MetroStars

1998 Joined the New York/New Jersey MetroStars

1997 Led his high school basketball team to the
conference championship
Played six games with the North Jersey Imperials

Glossary

clean sheets: games in which the opposing team doesn't score any goals

conference: a group of teams that play against one another

contract: a legal agreement that states how much a player will be paid and how long he will be with a team

draws: games that end with an even score

extra time: time added to the end of each half in a soccer game

goalkeeper: a soccer player whose job it is to keep the other team from scoring

pitch: a soccer field

Premier League: the top soccer league in England

save: to stop the opposing team from scoring by batting the ball away or catching the ball

tics: uncontrollable muscle movements

Tourette syndrome: a medical condition that causes uncontrollable muscle movements and sounds

Further Reading & Websites

Fishman, Jon M. *Abby Wambach*. Minneapolis: Lerner Publications, 2014.

Higgins, M. G. *Blow Out*. Minneapolis: Darby Creek, 2013.

Everton FC
http://www.evertonfc.com
Everton Football Club's official website is full of statistics, stories, videos, and much more.

Tim Howard/Everton FC
http://www.evertonfc.com/players/t/th/tim-howard
Tim's official Everton player page includes statistics, videos, and more about the team's goalkeeper.

US Soccer
http://www.ussoccer.com
The official website of US soccer has up-to-date information and stories about the US men's and women's soccer teams.

Index

Photo Acknowledgments

The images in this book are used with the permission of: © Adrian Dennis/AFP/Getty Images, p. 4; © Lars Baron/FIFA via Getty Images, pp. 5, 9 (right), 24; © Robert Cianflone/Getty Images, pp. 6, 8; © Kevin C. Cox/Getty Images, p. 7; © Carlos Becerra/Anadolu Agency/Getty Images, p. 9 (left); © Splash News/CORBIS, p. 10; © David Bergman/CORBIS, p. 11; Scott Bales/Icon SMI/Newscom, p. 12; © NBTHS Yearbook/Splash News/CORBIS, pp. 13, 15; © North Brunswick Township/Splash News/CORBIS, p. 14; © Ezra Shaw/ALLSPORT/Getty Images, p. 17; © Matthew Peters/Manchester United via Getty Images, p. 18; © Chris Coleman/Manchester United via Getty Images, p. 19; © Carl De Souza/AFP/Getty Images, p. 20; © Ian Kington/AFP/Getty Images, p. 21; © Gabriel Bouys/AFP/Getty Images, p. 22; © Jeff Mitchell/FIFA via Getty Images, p. 23; AP Photo/Kyodo, p. 25; © Odd Andersen/AFP/Getty Images, pp. 26, 29; AP Photo/Rex Features, p. 27; © John Todd/ISI/CORBIS, p. 28.

Front cover: © Lars Baron/FIFA/Getty Images.

Main body text set in Caecilia LT Std 55 Roman 16/28.
Typeface provided by Adobe Systems.